TRUST IN THE

LORD WITH ALL

YOUR HEART.

PROVERBS 3:5 ESV

Belle City Gifts
Savage, Minnesota, USA

Belle City Gifts is an imprint of BroadStreet Publishing Group LLC.
Broadstreetpublishing.com

Trust in the Lord 2021/2022 Planner

978-1-4245-6309-8

Design by Chris Garborg | garborgdesign.com
Compiled and edited by Michelle Winger | literallyprecise.com

Printed in China.

PERSONAL INFORMATION

Name ______________________

Address ______________________

____

____

____

Phone (h) ______________________

(w) ______________________

(c) ______________________

____

Email Address ______________________

____

Emergency Contacts ______________________

____

____

____

Family and Friends ______________________

____

____

____

____

____

____

____

____

____

____

2021 AT A GLANCE

JANUARY 2021

S	M	T	W	T	F	S
					1	2
3	4	5	6	7	8	9
10	11	12	13	14	15	16
17	18	19	20	21	22	23
24	25	26	27	28	29	30
31						

FEBRUARY 2021

S	M	T	W	T	F	S
	1	2	3	4	5	6
7	8	9	10	11	12	13
14	15	16	17	18	19	20
21	22	23	24	25	26	27
28						

MARCH 2021

S	M	T	W	T	F	S
	1	2	3	4	5	6
7	8	9	10	11	12	13
14	15	16	17	18	19	20
21	22	23	24	25	26	27
28	29	30	31			

APRIL 2021

S	M	T	W	T	F	S
				1	2	3
4	5	6	7	8	9	10
11	12	13	14	15	16	17
18	19	20	21	22	23	24
25	26	27	28	29	30	

MAY 2021

S	M	T	W	T	F	S
						1
2	3	4	5	6	7	8
9	10	11	12	13	14	15
16	17	18	19	20	21	22
23	24	25	26	27	28	29
30	31					

JUNE 2021

S	M	T	W	T	F	S
		1	2	3	4	5
6	7	8	9	10	11	12
13	14	15	16	17	18	19
20	21	22	23	24	25	26
27	28	29	30			

JULY 2021

S	M	T	W	T	F	S
				1	2	3
4	5	6	7	8	9	10
11	12	13	14	15	16	17
18	19	20	21	22	23	24
25	26	27	28	29	30	31

AUGUST 2021

S	M	T	W	T	F	S
1	2	3	4	5	6	7
8	9	10	11	12	13	14
15	16	17	18	19	20	21
22	23	24	25	26	27	28
29	30	31				

SEPTEMBER 2021

S	M	T	W	T	F	S
			1	2	3	4
5	6	7	8	9	10	11
12	13	14	15	16	17	18
19	20	21	22	23	24	25
26	27	28	29	30		

OCTOBER 2021

S	M	T	W	T	F	S
					1	2
3	4	5	6	7	8	9
10	11	12	13	14	15	16
17	18	19	20	21	22	23
24	25	26	27	28	29	30
31						

NOVEMBER 2021

S	M	T	W	T	F	S
	1	2	3	4	5	6
7	8	9	10	11	12	13
14	15	16	17	18	19	20
21	22	23	24	25	26	27
28	29	30				

DECEMBER 2021

S	M	T	W	T	F	S
			1	2	3	4
5	6	7	8	9	10	11
12	13	14	15	16	17	18
19	20	21	22	23	24	25
26	27	28	29	30	31	

2022 AT A GLANCE

JANUARY 2022

S	M	T	W	T	F	S
						1
2	3	4	5	6	7	8
9	10	11	12	13	14	15
16	17	18	19	20	21	22
23	24	25	26	27	28	29
30	31					

FEBRUARY 2022

S	M	T	W	T	F	S
		1	2	3	4	5
6	7	8	9	10	11	12
13	14	15	16	17	18	19
20	21	22	23	24	25	26
27	28					

MARCH 2022

S	M	T	W	T	F	S
		1	2	3	4	5
6	7	8	9	10	11	12
13	14	15	16	17	18	19
20	21	22	23	24	25	26
27	28	29	30	31		

APRIL 2022

S	M	T	W	T	F	S
					1	2
3	4	5	6	7	8	9
10	11	12	13	14	15	16
17	18	19	20	21	22	23
24	25	26	27	28	29	30

MAY 2022

S	M	T	W	T	F	S
1	2	3	4	5	6	7
8	9	10	11	12	13	14
15	16	17	18	19	20	21
22	23	24	25	26	27	28
29	30	31				

JUNE 2022

S	M	T	W	T	F	S
			1	2	3	4
5	6	7	8	9	10	11
12	13	14	15	16	17	18
19	20	21	22	23	24	25
26	27	28	29	30		

JULY 2022

S	M	T	W	T	F	S
					1	2
3	4	5	6	7	8	9
10	11	12	13	14	15	16
17	18	19	20	21	22	23
24	25	26	27	28	29	30
31						

AUGUST 2022

S	M	T	W	T	F	S
	1	2	3	4	5	6
7	8	9	10	11	12	13
14	15	16	17	18	19	20
21	22	23	24	25	26	27
28	29	30	31			

SEPTEMBER 2022

S	M	T	W	T	F	S
				1	2	3
4	5	6	7	8	9	10
11	12	13	14	15	16	17
18	19	20	21	22	23	24
25	26	27	28	29	30	

OCTOBER 2022

S	M	T	W	T	F	S
						1
2	3	4	5	6	7	8
9	10	11	12	13	14	15
16	17	18	19	20	21	22
23	24	25	26	27	28	29
30	31					

NOVEMBER 2022

S	M	T	W	T	F	S
		1	2	3	4	5
6	7	8	9	10	11	12
13	14	15	16	17	18	19
20	21	22	23	24	25	26
27	28	29	30			

DECEMBER 2022

S	M	T	W	T	F	S
				1	2	3
4	5	6	7	8	9	10
11	12	13	14	15	16	17
18	19	20	21	22	23	24
25	26	27	28	29	30	31

Important Dates

JULY–DECEMBER 2021

Independence Day	July 4
Labor Day	September 6
Autumnal Equinox	September 22
Daylight Saving Time Ends	November 7
Veterans Day	November 11
Thanksgiving Day	November 25
First Sunday of Advent	November 28
Hanukkah Begins	November 28
Hanukkah Ends	December 6
Winter Solstice	December 21
Christmas Eve	December 24
Christmas Day	December 25
New Year's Eve	December 31

JANUARY–DECEMBER 2022

New Year's Day	January 1
Martin Luther King Jr. Day	January 17
Valentine's Day	February 14
Presidents' Day	February 21
Daylight Saving Time begins	March 13
St. Patrick's Day	March 17

Spring Equinox	March 20
Palm Sunday	April 10
Good Friday	April 15
Easter Sunday	April 17
National Day of Prayer	May 5
Mother's Day	May 8
Memorial Day	May 30
Summer Solstice	June 21
Father's Day	June 19
Independence Day	July 4
Labor Day	September 5
Autumnal Equinox	September 22
Daylight Saving Time Ends	November 6
Veterans Day	November 11
Thanksgiving Day	November 24
First Sunday of Advent	November 27
Hanukkah Begins	December 18
Winter Solstice	December 21
Christmas Eve	December 24
Christmas Day	December 25
Hanukkah Ends	December 26
New Year's Eve	December 31

2021

July

Take delight in the Lord,
and he will give you your heart's desires.
Commit everything you do to the Lord.
Trust him, and he will help you.

PSALM 37:4-5 NLT

My Goals for the Month

JULY AT A GLANCE

Sun	Mon	Tue	Wed	Thu	Fri	Sat
				1	2	3
4	5	6	7	8	9	10
11	12	13	14	15	16	17
18	19	20	21	22	23	24
25	26	27	28	29	30	31

JUNE/ JULY

JULY 2021

S	M	T	W	T	F	S
				1	2	3
4	5	6	7	8	9	10
11	12	13	14	15	16	17
18	19	20	21	22	23	24
25	26	27	28	29	30	31

AUGUST 2021

S	M	T	W	T	F	S
1	2	3	4	5	6	7
8	9	10	11	12	13	14
15	16	17	18	19	20	21
22	23	24	25	26	27	28
29	30	31				

Prayer List

MONDAY 28

TUESDAY 29

WEDNESDAY 30

Priorities

I'm thankful for...

You, O LORD, will bless the righteous;
With favor You will surround him
as with a shield.

PSALM 5:12 NKJV

THURSDAY 1	FRIDAY 2	SATURDAY 3	SUNDAY 4

JULY

JULY 2021						
S	M	T	W	T	F	S
				1	2	3
4	5	6	7	8	9	10
11	12	13	14	15	16	17
18	19	20	21	22	23	24
25	26	27	28	29	30	31

AUGUST 2021						
S	M	T	W	T	F	S
1	2	3	4	5	6	7
8	9	10	11	12	13	14
15	16	17	18	19	20	21
22	23	24	25	26	27	28
29	30	31				

Prayer List

Priorities

MONDAY 5

TUESDAY 6

WEDNESDAY 7

I'm thankful for...

I can do everything through Christ,
who gives me strength.

PHILIPPIANS 4:13 NLT

THURSDAY 8	FRIDAY 9	SATURDAY 10	SUNDAY 11

JULY

JULY 2021						
S	M	T	W	T	F	S
				1	2	3
4	5	6	7	8	9	10
11	12	13	14	15	16	17
18	19	20	21	22	23	24
25	26	27	28	29	30	31

AUGUST 2021						
S	M	T	W	T	F	S
1	2	3	4	5	6	7
8	9	10	11	12	13	14
15	16	17	18	19	20	21
22	23	24	25	26	27	28
29	30	31				

Prayer List

MONDAY 12

TUESDAY 13

WEDNESDAY 14

Priorities

I'm thankful for...

The Lord will be your confidence,
And will keep your foot
from being caught.

PROVERBS 3:26 NKJV

THURSDAY 15	FRIDAY 16	SATURDAY 17	SUNDAY 18

JULY

JULY 2021						
S	M	T	W	T	F	S
				1	2	3
4	5	6	7	8	9	10
11	12	13	14	15	16	17
18	19	20	21	22	23	24
25	26	27	28	29	30	31

AUGUST 2021						
S	M	T	W	T	F	S
1	2	3	4	5	6	7
8	9	10	11	12	13	14
15	16	17	18	19	20	21
22	23	24	25	26	27	28
29	30	31				

Prayer List

MONDAY 19

TUESDAY 20

WEDNESDAY 21

Priorities

I'm thankful for...

For we are God's masterpiece. He has created us anew in Christ Jesus, so we can do the good things he planned for us long ago.

EPHESIANS 2:10 NLT

THURSDAY 22	FRIDAY 23	SATURDAY 24	SUNDAY 25

JULY/ AUGUST

JULY 2021

S	M	T	W	T	F	S
				1	2	3
4	5	6	7	8	9	10
11	12	13	14	15	16	17
18	19	20	21	22	23	24
25	26	27	28	29	30	31

AUGUST 2021

S	M	T	W	T	F	S
1	2	3	4	5	6	7
8	9	10	11	12	13	14
15	16	17	18	19	20	21
22	23	24	25	26	27	28
29	30	31				

Prayer List

MONDAY 26

TUESDAY 27

WEDNESDAY 28

Priorities

I'm thankful for...

Even when I walk
through the darkest valley,
I will not be afraid,
for you are close beside me.

PSALM 23:4 NLT

THURSDAY 29	FRIDAY 30	SATURDAY 31	SUNDAY 1

To Do

2021

August

Blessed be the God and Father of our Lord Jesus Christ, who has blessed us in Christ with every spiritual blessing in the heavenly places, even as he chose us in him before the foundation of the world, that we should be holy and blameless before him.

EPHESIANS 1:3-4 ESV

My Goals for the Month

AUGUST AT A GLANCE

Sun	Mon	Tue	Wed	Thu	Fri	Sat
1	2	3	4	5	6	7
8	9	10	11	12	13	14
15	16	17	18	19	20	21
22	23	24	25	26	27	28
29	30	31				

AUGUST

AUGUST 2021

S	M	T	W	T	F	S
1	2	3	4	5	6	7
8	9	10	11	12	13	14
15	16	17	18	19	20	21
22	23	24	25	26	27	28
29	30	31				

SEPTEMBER 2021

S	M	T	W	T	F	S
			1	2	3	4
5	6	7	8	9	10	11
12	13	14	15	16	17	18
19	20	21	22	23	24	25
26	27	28	29	30		

Prayer List

MONDAY 2

TUESDAY 3

WEDNESDAY 4

Priorities

I'm thankful for...

Let your speech always be with grace,
as though seasoned with salt,
so that you will know how you
should respond to each person.

COLOSSIANS 4:6 NASB

THURSDAY 5	FRIDAY 6	SATURDAY 7	SUNDAY 8

AUGUST

AUGUST 2021

S	M	T	W	T	F	S
1	2	3	4	5	6	7
8	9	10	11	12	13	14
15	16	17	18	19	20	21
22	23	24	25	26	27	28
29	30	31				

SEPTEMBER 2021

S	M	T	W	T	F	S
			1	2	3	4
5	6	7	8	9	10	11
12	13	14	15	16	17	18
19	20	21	22	23	24	25
26	27	28	29	30		

Prayer List	MONDAY 9	TUESDAY 10	WEDNESDAY 11

Priorities

I'm thankful for...

The heavens are telling
of the glory of God;
And their expanse is declaring
the work of His hands.

PSALM 19:1 NASB

THURSDAY 12	FRIDAY 13	SATURDAY 14	SUNDAY 15

AUGUST

AUGUST 2021						
S	M	T	W	T	F	S
1	2	3	4	5	6	7
8	9	10	11	12	13	14
15	16	17	18	19	20	21
22	23	24	25	26	27	28
29	30	31				

SEPTEMBER 2021						
S	M	T	W	T	F	S
			1	2	3	4
5	6	7	8	9	10	11
12	13	14	15	16	17	18
19	20	21	22	23	24	25
26	27	28	29	30		

Prayer List

MONDAY 16

TUESDAY 17

WEDNESDAY 18

Priorities

I'm thankful for...

Why am I so sad?
Why am I so upset?
I should put my hope in God
and keep praising him.

PSALM 42:11 NCV

THURSDAY 19	FRIDAY 20	SATURDAY 21	SUNDAY 22

AUGUST

AUGUST 2021						
S	M	T	W	T	F	S
1	2	3	4	5	6	7
8	9	10	11	12	13	14
15	16	17	18	19	20	21
22	23	24	25	26	27	28
29	30	31				

SEPTEMBER 2021						
S	M	T	W	T	F	S
			1	2	3	4
5	6	7	8	9	10	11
12	13	14	15	16	17	18
19	20	21	22	23	24	25
26	27	28	29	30		

Prayer List

MONDAY 23

TUESDAY 24

WEDNESDAY 25

Priorities

I'm thankful for...

Do your best to present yourself
to God as one approved by him,
a worker who has no need
to be ashamed, rightly explaining
the word of truth.

2 TIMOTHY 2:15 NRSV

THURSDAY 26	FRIDAY 27	SATURDAY 28	SUNDAY 29

To Do

2021

September

I will sing of the LORD's great love forever;
with my mouth I will make your faithfulness known
through all generations. I will declare that your love
stands firm forever,that you have established your
faithfulness in heaven itself.

PSALM 89:1-2 NIV

My Goals for the Month

SEPTEMBER AT A GLANCE

Sun	Mon	Tue	Wed	Thu	Fri	Sat
			1	2	3	4
5	6	7	8	9	10	11
12	13	14	15	16	17	18
19	20	21	22	23	24	25
26	27	28	29	30		

AUGUST/ SEPTEMBER

SEPTEMBER 2021

S	M	T	W	T	F	S
			1	2	3	4
5	6	7	8	9	10	11
12	13	14	15	16	17	18
19	20	21	22	23	24	25
26	27	28	29	30		

OCTOBER 2021

S	M	T	W	T	F	S
					1	2
3	4	5	6	7	8	9
10	11	12	13	14	15	16
17	18	19	20	21	22	23
24	25	26	27	28	29	30
31						

Prayer List	MONDAY 30	TUESDAY 31	WEDNESDAY 1
Priorities			

I'm thankful for...

Before the mountains were brought
forth, or ever you had formed
the earth and the world,
from everlasting to everlasting
you are God.

PSALM 90:2 ESV

THURSDAY 2	FRIDAY 3	SATURDAY 4	SUNDAY 5

SEPTEMBER

SEPTEMBER 2021						
S	M	T	W	T	F	S
			1	2	3	4
5	6	7	8	9	10	11
12	13	14	15	16	17	18
19	20	21	22	23	24	25
26	27	28	29	30		

OCTOBER 2021						
S	M	T	W	T	F	S
					1	2
3	4	5	6	7	8	9
10	11	12	13	14	15	16
17	18	19	20	21	22	23
24	25	26	27	28	29	30
31						

Prayer List

MONDAY 6

TUESDAY 7

WEDNESDAY 8

Priorities

I'm thankful for...

It is my prayer that your love may abound more and more, with knowledge and all discernment, so that you may approve what is excellent, and so be pure and blameless for the day of Christ.

PHILIPPIANS 1:9-10 ESV

THURSDAY 9	FRIDAY 10	SATURDAY 11	SUNDAY 12

SEPTEMBER

SEPTEMBER 2021

S	M	T	W	T	F	S
			1	2	3	4
5	6	7	8	9	10	11
12	13	14	15	16	17	18
19	20	21	22	23	24	25
26	27	28	29	30		

OCTOBER 2021

S	M	T	W	T	F	S
					1	2
3	4	5	6	7	8	9
10	11	12	13	14	15	16
17	18	19	20	21	22	23
24	25	26	27	28	29	30
31						

Prayer List

Priorities

MONDAY 13

TUESDAY 14

WEDNESDAY 15

I'm thankful for...

The law of the Lord is perfect,
refreshing the soul.

PSALM 19:7 NIV

THURSDAY 16	FRIDAY 17	SATURDAY 18	SUNDAY 19

SEPTEMBER

SEPTEMBER 2021						
S	M	T	W	T	F	S
			1	2	3	4
5	6	7	8	9	10	11
12	13	14	15	16	17	18
19	20	21	22	23	24	25
26	27	28	29	30		

OCTOBER 2021						
S	M	T	W	T	F	S
					1	2
3	4	5	6	7	8	9
10	11	12	13	14	15	16
17	18	19	20	21	22	23
24	25	26	27	28	29	30
31						

Prayer List

MONDAY 20

TUESDAY 21

WEDNESDAY 22

Priorities

I'm thankful for...

Whether you eat or drink,
or whatever you do,
do all to the glory of God.

1 CORINTHIANS 10:31 NKJV

THURSDAY 23	FRIDAY 24	SATURDAY 25	SUNDAY 26

To Do

2021

October

The LORD your God is in your midst,
a mighty one who will save;
he will rejoice over you with gladness;
he will quiet you by his love;
he will exult over you with loud singing.

ZEPHANIAH 3:17 ESV

My Goals for the Month

OCTOBER AT A GLANCE

Sun	Mon	Tue	Wed	Thu	Fri	Sat
					1	2
3	4	5	6	7	8	9
10	11	12	13	14	15	16
17	18	19	20	21	22	23
24 / 31	25	26	27	28	29	30

SEPTEMBER/ OCTOBER

OCTOBER 2021						
S	M	T	W	T	F	S
					1	2
3	4	5	6	7	8	9
10	11	12	13	14	15	16
17	18	19	20	21	22	23
24	25	26	27	28	29	30
31						

NOVEMBER 2021						
S	M	T	W	T	F	S
	1	2	3	4	5	6
7	8	9	10	11	12	13
14	15	16	17	18	19	20
21	22	23	24	25	26	27
28	29	30				

Prayer List

Priorities

MONDAY 27

TUESDAY 28

WEDNESDAY 29

I'm thankful for...

For the word of the Lord is upright,
and all his work is done
in faithfulness.

PSALM 33:4 ESV

THURSDAY 30	FRIDAY 1	SATURDAY 2	SUNDAY 3

OCTOBER

OCTOBER 2021						
S	M	T	W	T	F	S
					1	2
3	4	5	6	7	8	9
10	11	12	13	14	15	16
17	18	19	20	21	22	23
24	25	26	27	28	29	30
31						

NOVEMBER 2021						
S	M	T	W	T	F	S
	1	2	3	4	5	6
7	8	9	10	11	12	13
14	15	16	17	18	19	20
21	22	23	24	25	26	27
28	29	30				

Prayer List	MONDAY 4	TUESDAY 5	WEDNESDAY 6

Priorities

I'm thankful for...

When you lie down,
you will not be afraid;
when you lie down,
your sleep will be sweet.

PROVERBS 3:24 NIV

THURSDAY 7	FRIDAY 8	SATURDAY 9	SUNDAY 10

OCTOBER

OCTOBER 2021						
S	M	T	W	T	F	S
					1	2
3	4	5	6	7	8	9
10	11	12	13	14	15	16
17	18	19	20	21	22	23
24	25	26	27	28	29	30
31						

NOVEMBER 2021						
S	M	T	W	T	F	S
	1	2	3	4	5	6
7	8	9	10	11	12	13
14	15	16	17	18	19	20
21	22	23	24	25	26	27
28	29	30				

Prayer List

Priorities

MONDAY 11

TUESDAY 12

WEDNESDAY 13

I'm thankful for...

God is our refuge and strength,
an ever-present help in trouble.

PSALM 46:1-3 NIV

THURSDAY 14	FRIDAY 15	SATURDAY 16	SUNDAY 17

OCTOBER

OCTOBER 2021						
S	M	T	W	T	F	S
					1	2
3	4	5	6	7	8	9
10	11	12	13	14	15	16
17	18	19	20	21	22	23
24	25	26	27	28	29	30
31						

NOVEMBER 2021						
S	M	T	W	T	F	S
	1	2	3	4	5	6
7	8	9	10	11	12	13
14	15	16	17	18	19	20
21	22	23	24	25	26	27
28	29	30				

Prayer List	MONDAY 18	TUESDAY 19	WEDNESDAY 20

Priorities

I'm thankful for...

For You, LORD, are good,
and ready to forgive,
And abundant in mercy
to all those who call upon You.

PSALM 86:5 NKJV

THURSDAY 21	FRIDAY 22	SATURDAY 23	SUNDAY 24

OCTOBER

OCTOBER 2021

S	M	T	W	T	F	S
					1	2
3	4	5	6	7	8	9
10	11	12	13	14	15	16
17	18	19	20	21	22	23
24	25	26	27	28	29	30
31						

NOVEMBER 2021

S	M	T	W	T	F	S
	1	2	3	4	5	6
7	8	9	10	11	12	13
14	15	16	17	18	19	20
21	22	23	24	25	26	27
28	29	30				

Prayer List	MONDAY 25	TUESDAY 26	WEDNESDAY 27

Priorities

I'm thankful for...

Taste and see that
the LORD is good;
blessed is the one
who takes refuge in him.

PSALM 34:8 NIV

THURSDAY 28	FRIDAY 29	SATURDAY 30	SUNDAY 31

To Do

2021

November

You created my inmost being;
you knit me together in my mother's womb.
I praise you because I am fearfully
and wonderfully made;
your works are wonderful,
I know that full well.

PSALM 139:13-14 NIV

My Goals for the Month

NOVEMBER AT A GLANCE

Sun	Mon	Tue	Wed	Thu	Fri	Sat
	1	2	3	4	5	6
7	8	9	10	11	12	13
14	15	16	17	18	19	20
21	22	23	24	25	26	27
28	29	30				

NOVEMBER

NOVEMBER 2021						
S	M	T	W	T	F	S
	1	2	3	4	5	6
7	8	9	10	11	12	13
14	15	16	17	18	19	20
21	22	23	24	25	26	27
28	29	30				

DECEMBER 2021						
S	M	T	W	T	F	S
			1	2	3	4
5	6	7	8	9	10	11
12	13	14	15	16	17	18
19	20	21	22	23	24	25
26	27	28	29	30	31	

Prayer List	MONDAY 1	TUESDAY 2	WEDNESDAY 3

Priorities

I'm thankful for...

The Lord is good to all,
and his mercy is over all
that he has made.

PSALM 145:9 ESV

THURSDAY 4	FRIDAY 5	SATURDAY 6	SUNDAY 7

NOVEMBER

NOVEMBER 2021						
S	M	T	W	T	F	S
	1	2	3	4	5	6
7	8	9	10	11	12	13
14	15	16	17	18	19	20
21	22	23	24	25	26	27
28	29	30				

DECEMBER 2021						
S	M	T	W	T	F	S
			1	2	3	4
5	6	7	8	9	10	11
12	13	14	15	16	17	18
19	20	21	22	23	24	25
26	27	28	29	30	31	

Prayer List

MONDAY 8

TUESDAY 9

WEDNESDAY 10

Priorities

I'm thankful for...

Those who deal truthfully are His delight.

PROVERBS 12:22 NKJV

THURSDAY 11	FRIDAY 12	SATURDAY 13	SUNDAY 14

NOVEMBER

NOVEMBER 2021

S	M	T	W	T	F	S
	1	2	3	4	5	6
7	8	9	10	11	12	13
14	15	16	17	18	19	20
21	22	23	24	25	26	27
28	29	30				

DECEMBER 2021

S	M	T	W	T	F	S
			1	2	3	4
5	6	7	8	9	10	11
12	13	14	15	16	17	18
19	20	21	22	23	24	25
26	27	28	29	30	31	

Prayer List

MONDAY 15

TUESDAY 16

WEDNESDAY 17

Priorities

I'm thankful for...

Sing to the LORD with thanksgiving.
He covers the heavens with clouds;
he prepares rain for the earth, and
makes grass grow on the hills.

PSALM 147:8 ESV

THURSDAY 18	FRIDAY 19	SATURDAY 20	SUNDAY 21

NOVEMBER

NOVEMBER 2021						
S	M	T	W	T	F	S
	1	2	3	4	5	6
7	8	9	10	11	12	13
14	15	16	17	18	19	20
21	22	23	24	25	26	27
28	29	30				

DECEMBER 2021						
S	M	T	W	T	F	S
			1	2	3	4
5	6	7	8	9	10	11
12	13	14	15	16	17	18
19	20	21	22	23	24	25
26	27	28	29	30	31	

Prayer List

MONDAY 22

TUESDAY 23

WEDNESDAY 24

Priorities

I'm thankful for...

The LORD takes pleasure
in those who fear Him,
In those who hope in His mercy.

PSALM 147:11 NKJV

THURSDAY 25	FRIDAY 26	SATURDAY 27	SUNDAY 28

To Do

2021

December

Consider it pure joy, my brothers and sisters,
whenever you face trials of many kinds,
because you know that the testing of
your faith produces perseverance.

JAMES 1:2-3 NIV

My Goals for the Month

DECEMBER AT A GLANCE

Sun	Mon	Tue	Wed	Thu	Fri	Sat
			1	2	3	4
5	6	7	8	9	10	11
12	13	14	15	16	17	18
19	20	21	22	23	24	25
26	27	28	29	30	31	

NOVEMBER/ DECEMBER

DECEMBER 2021

S	M	T	W	T	F	S
			1	2	3	4
5	6	7	8	9	10	11
12	13	14	15	16	17	18
19	20	21	22	23	24	25
26	27	28	29	30	31	

JANUARY 2022

S	M	T	W	T	F	S
						1
2	3	4	5	6	7	8
9	10	11	12	13	14	15
16	17	18	19	20	21	22
23	24	25	26	27	28	29
30	31					

Prayer List	MONDAY 29	TUESDAY 30	WEDNESDAY 1

Priorities

I'm thankful for...

The precepts of the LORD are right,
giving joy to the heart.
The commands of the LORD are
radiant, giving light to the eyes.

PSALM 19:8 NIV

THURSDAY 2	FRIDAY 3	SATURDAY 4	SUNDAY 5

DECEMBER

DECEMBER 2021

S	M	T	W	T	F	S
			1	2	3	4
5	6	7	8	9	10	11
12	13	14	15	16	17	18
19	20	21	22	23	24	25
26	27	28	29	30	31	

JANUARY 2022

S	M	T	W	T	F	S
						1
2	3	4	5	6	7	8
9	10	11	12	13	14	15
16	17	18	19	20	21	22
23	24	25	26	27	28	29
30	31					

Prayer List

MONDAY 6

TUESDAY 7

WEDNESDAY 8

Priorities

I'm thankful for...

Because of my integrity
you uphold me and set me
in your presence forever.

PSALM 41:12 NIV

THURSDAY 9	FRIDAY 10	SATURDAY 11	SUNDAY 12

DECEMBER

DECEMBER 2021						
S	M	T	W	T	F	S
			1	2	3	4
5	6	7	8	9	10	11
12	13	14	15	16	17	18
19	20	21	22	23	24	25
26	27	28	29	30	31	

JANUARY 2022						
S	M	T	W	T	F	S
						1
2	3	4	5	6	7	8
9	10	11	12	13	14	15
16	17	18	19	20	21	22
23	24	25	26	27	28	29
30	31					

Prayer List	MONDAY 13	TUESDAY 14	WEDNESDAY 15
Priorities			

I'm thankful for...

For His merciful kindness
is great toward us,
And the truth of the Lord
endures forever.

PSALM 117:2 NKJV

THURSDAY 16	FRIDAY 17	SATURDAY 18	SUNDAY 19

DECEMBER

DECEMBER 2021

S	M	T	W	T	F	S
			1	2	3	4
5	6	7	8	9	10	11
12	13	14	15	16	17	18
19	20	21	22	23	24	25
26	27	28	29	30	31	

JANUARY 2022

S	M	T	W	T	F	S
						1
2	3	4	5	6	7	8
9	10	11	12	13	14	15
16	17	18	19	20	21	22
23	24	25	26	27	28	29
30	31					

Prayer List	MONDAY 20	TUESDAY 21	WEDNESDAY 22

Priorities

I'm thankful for...

Three things will last forever—
faith, hope, and love—
and the greatest of these is love.

1 CORINTHIANS 13:13 NLT

THURSDAY 23	FRIDAY 24	SATURDAY 25	SUNDAY 26

DECEMBER/ JANUARY

DECEMBER 2021

S	M	T	W	T	F	S
			1	2	3	4
5	6	7	8	9	10	11
12	13	14	15	16	17	18
19	20	21	22	23	24	25
26	27	28	29	30	31	

JANUARY 2022

S	M	T	W	T	F	S
						1
2	3	4	5	6	7	8
9	10	11	12	13	14	15
16	17	18	19	20	21	22
23	24	25	26	27	28	29
30	31					

Prayer List	MONDAY 27	TUESDAY 28	WEDNESDAY 29

Priorities

I'm thankful for...

They who wait for the LORD shall renew their strength; they shall mount up with wings like eagles; they shall run and not be weary; they shall walk and not faint.

ISAIAH 40:31 ESV

THURSDAY 30	FRIDAY 31	SATURDAY 1	SUNDAY 2

To Do

2022

January

We do not lose heart, but though our outer man is decaying, yet our inner man is being renewed day by day. For momentary, light affliction is producing for us an eternal weight of glory far beyond all comparison.

2 CORINTHIANS 4:16-17 NASB

My Goals for the Month

JANUARY AT A GLANCE

Sun	Mon	Tue	Wed	Thu	Fri	Sat
						1
2	3	4	5	6	7	8
9	10	11	12	13	14	15
16	17	18	19	20	21	22
23 / 30	24 / 31	25	26	27	28	29

JANUARY

JANUARY 2022

S	M	T	W	T	F	S
						1
2	3	4	5	6	7	8
9	10	11	12	13	14	15
16	17	18	19	20	21	22
23	24	25	26	27	28	29
30	31					

FEBRUARY 2022

S	M	T	W	T	F	S
		1	2	3	4	5
6	7	8	9	10	11	12
13	14	15	16	17	18	19
20	21	22	23	24	25	26
27	28					

Prayer List

MONDAY 3

TUESDAY 4

WEDNESDAY 5

Priorities

I'm thankful for...

Always give yourselves fully
to the work of the Lord,
because you know that your
labor in the Lord is not in vain.

1 CORINTHIANS 15:58 NIV

THURSDAY 6	FRIDAY 7	SATURDAY 8	SUNDAY 9

JANUARY

JANUARY 2022

S	M	T	W	T	F	S
						1
2	3	4	5	6	7	8
9	10	11	12	13	14	15
16	17	18	19	20	21	22
23	24	25	26	27	28	29
30	31					

FEBRUARY 2022

S	M	T	W	T	F	S
		1	2	3	4	5
6	7	8	9	10	11	12
13	14	15	16	17	18	19
20	21	22	23	24	25	26
27	28					

Prayer List	MONDAY 10	TUESDAY 11	WEDNESDAY 12

Priorities

I'm thankful for...

The Lord is for me; he will help me.
It is better to take refuge in the Lord
than to trust in people.

PSALM 118:7-8 NLT

THURSDAY 13	FRIDAY 14	SATURDAY 15	SUNDAY 16

JANUARY

JANUARY 2022						
S	M	T	W	T	F	S
						1
2	3	4	5	6	7	8
9	10	11	12	13	14	15
16	17	18	19	20	21	22
23	24	25	26	27	28	29
30	31					

FEBRUARY 2022						
S	M	T	W	T	F	S
		1	2	3	4	5
6	7	8	9	10	11	12
13	14	15	16	17	18	19
20	21	22	23	24	25	26
27	28					

Prayer List	MONDAY 17	TUESDAY 18	WEDNESDAY 19

Priorities

I'm thankful for...

I keep my eyes always on the LORD.
With him at my right hand,
I will not be shaken.

PSALM 16:8 NIV

THURSDAY 20	FRIDAY 21	SATURDAY 22	SUNDAY 23

JANUARY

JANUARY 2022						
S	M	T	W	T	F	S
						1
2	3	4	5	6	7	8
9	10	11	12	13	14	15
16	17	18	19	20	21	22
23	24	25	26	27	28	29
30	31					

FEBRUARY 2022						
S	M	T	W	T	F	S
		1	2	3	4	5
6	7	8	9	10	11	12
13	14	15	16	17	18	19
20	21	22	23	24	25	26
27	28					

Prayer List

Priorities

MONDAY 24

TUESDAY 25

WEDNESDAY 26

I'm thankful for...

Blessed is the one who finds wisdom,
and the one who gets understanding.

PROVERBS 3:13 ESV

THURSDAY 27	FRIDAY 28	SATURDAY 29	SUNDAY 30

To Do

2022

February

With me are riches and honor,
enduring wealth and prosperity.
My fruit is better than fine gold;
what I yield surpasses choice silver.

PROVERBS 8:18-19 NIV

My Goals for the Month

FEBRUARY AT A GLANCE

Sun	Mon	Tue	Wed	Thu	Fri	Sat
		1	2	3	4	5
6	7	8	9	10	11	12
13	14	15	16	17	18	19
20	21	22	23	24	25	26
27	28					

JANUARY/ FEBRUARY

FEBRUARY 2022						
S	M	T	W	T	F	S
		1	2	3	4	5
6	7	8	9	10	11	12
13	14	15	16	17	18	19
20	21	22	23	24	25	26
27	28					

MARCH 2022						
S	M	T	W	T	F	S
		1	2	3	4	5
6	7	8	9	10	11	12
13	14	15	16	17	18	19
20	21	22	23	24	25	26
27	28	29	30	31		

Prayer List	MONDAY 31	TUESDAY 1	WEDNESDAY 2

Priorities

I'm thankful for...

Oh, the depth of the riches both of the wisdom and knowledge of God! How unsearchable are His judgments and unfathomable His ways!

ROMANS 11:33 NASB

THURSDAY 3	FRIDAY 4	SATURDAY 5	SUNDAY 6

FEBRUARY

FEBRUARY 2022						
S	M	T	W	T	F	S
		1	2	3	4	5
6	7	8	9	10	11	12
13	14	15	16	17	18	19
20	21	22	23	24	25	26
27	28					

MARCH 2022						
S	M	T	W	T	F	S
		1	2	3	4	5
6	7	8	9	10	11	12
13	14	15	16	17	18	19
20	21	22	23	24	25	26
27	28	29	30	31		

Prayer List

MONDAY 7

TUESDAY 8

WEDNESDAY 9

Priorities

I'm thankful for...

Give your burdens to the LORD,
and he will take care of you.
He will not permit the godly
to slip and fall.

PSALM 55:22 NLT

THURSDAY 10	FRIDAY 11	SATURDAY 12	SUNDAY 13

FEBRUARY

FEBRUARY 2022						
S	M	T	W	T	F	S
		1	2	3	4	5
6	7	8	9	10	11	12
13	14	15	16	17	18	19
20	21	22	23	24	25	26
27	28					

MARCH 2022						
S	M	T	W	T	F	S
		1	2	3	4	5
6	7	8	9	10	11	12
13	14	15	16	17	18	19
20	21	22	23	24	25	26
27	28	29	30	31		

Prayer List

MONDAY 14

TUESDAY 15

WEDNESDAY 16

Priorities

I'm thankful for...

You will experience God's peace, which exceeds anything we can understand. His peace will guard your hearts and minds as you live in Christ Jesus.

PHILIPPIANS 4:7 NLT

THURSDAY 17	FRIDAY 18	SATURDAY 19	SUNDAY 20

FEBRUARY

FEBRUARY 2022						
S	M	T	W	T	F	S
		1	2	3	4	5
6	7	8	9	10	11	12
13	14	15	16	17	18	19
20	21	22	23	24	25	26
27	28					

MARCH 2022						
S	M	T	W	T	F	S
		1	2	3	4	5
6	7	8	9	10	11	12
13	14	15	16	17	18	19
20	21	22	23	24	25	26
27	28	29	30	31		

Prayer List	MONDAY 21	TUESDAY 22	WEDNESDAY 23

Priorities

I'm thankful for...

Be still, and know that I am God;
I will be exalted among the nations,
I will be exalted in the earth!

PSALM 46:10 NKJV

THURSDAY 24	FRIDAY 25	SATURDAY 26	SUNDAY 27

To Do

2022

March

"You are the light of the world. A city set on a hill cannot be hidden. Nor do people light a lamp and put it under a basket, but on a stand, and it gives light to all in the house. In the same way, let your light shine before others, so that they may see your good works and give glory to your Father who is in heaven."

MATTHEW 5:14-16 ESV

My Goals for the Month

....

....

....

....

....

MARCH AT A GLANCE

Sun	Mon	Tue	Wed	Thu	Fri	Sat
		1	2	3	4	5
6	7	8	9	10	11	12
13	14	15	16	17	18	19
20	21	22	23	24	25	26
27	28	29	30	31		

FEBRUARY/ MARCH

MARCH 2022						
S	M	T	W	T	F	S
		1	2	3	4	5
6	7	8	9	10	11	12
13	14	15	16	17	18	19
20	21	22	23	24	25	26
27	28	29	30	31		

APRIL 2022						
S	M	T	W	T	F	S
					1	2
3	4	5	6	7	8	9
10	11	12	13	14	15	16
17	18	19	20	21	22	23
24	25	26	27	28	29	30

Prayer List

MONDAY 28

TUESDAY 1

WEDNESDAY 2

Priorities

I'm thankful for...

Let the sea and everything in it
shout his praise!
Let the earth and all
living things join in.

PSALM 98:7 NLT

THURSDAY 3	FRIDAY 4	SATURDAY 5	SUNDAY 6

MARCH

MARCH 2022

S	M	T	W	T	F	S
		1	2	3	4	5
6	7	8	9	10	11	12
13	14	15	16	17	18	19
20	21	22	23	24	25	26
27	28	29	30	31		

APRIL 2022

S	M	T	W	T	F	S
					1	2
3	4	5	6	7	8	9
10	11	12	13	14	15	16
17	18	19	20	21	22	23
24	25	26	27	28	29	30

Prayer List

MONDAY 7

TUESDAY 8

WEDNESDAY 9

Priorities

I'm thankful for...

I lie awake at night thinking of you—
of how much you have helped me—
and how I rejoice through the night
beneath the protecting shadow
of your wings.

PSALM 63:6-7 TLB

THURSDAY 10	FRIDAY 11	SATURDAY 12	SUNDAY 13

MARCH

MARCH 2022						
S	M	T	W	T	F	S
		1	2	3	4	5
6	7	8	9	10	11	12
13	14	15	16	17	18	19
20	21	22	23	24	25	26
27	28	29	30	31		

APRIL 2022						
S	M	T	W	T	F	S
					1	2
3	4	5	6	7	8	9
10	11	12	13	14	15	16
17	18	19	20	21	22	23
24	25	26	27	28	29	30

Prayer List

MONDAY 14

TUESDAY 15

WEDNESDAY 16

Priorities

I'm thankful for...

We can make our plans,
but the final outcome
is in God's hands.

PROVERBS 16:1 TLB

THURSDAY 17	FRIDAY 18	SATURDAY 19	SUNDAY 20

MARCH

MARCH 2022						
S	M	T	W	T	F	S
		1	2	3	4	5
6	7	8	9	10	11	12
13	14	15	16	17	18	19
20	21	22	23	24	25	26
27	28	29	30	31		

APRIL 2022						
S	M	T	W	T	F	S
					1	2
3	4	5	6	7	8	9
10	11	12	13	14	15	16
17	18	19	20	21	22	23
24	25	26	27	28	29	30

Prayer List	MONDAY 21	TUESDAY 22	WEDNESDAY 23

Priorities

I'm thankful for...

My child, don't lose sight of
common sense and discernment.
Hang on to them, for they
will refresh your soul.

PROVERBS 3:21-22 NLT

THURSDAY 24	FRIDAY 25	SATURDAY 26	SUNDAY 27

MARCH/ APRIL

MARCH 2022						
S	M	T	W	T	F	S
		1	2	3	4	5
6	7	8	9	10	11	12
13	14	15	16	17	18	19
20	21	22	23	24	25	26
27	28	29	30	31		

APRIL 2022						
S	M	T	W	T	F	S
					1	2
3	4	5	6	7	8	9
10	11	12	13	14	15	16
17	18	19	20	21	22	23
24	25	26	27	28	29	30

Prayer List	MONDAY 28	TUESDAY 29	WEDNESDAY 30

Priorities

I'm thankful for...

The steadfast love
of the LORD never ceases;
his mercies never come to an end.

LAMENTATIONS 3:22 ESV

THURSDAY 31	FRIDAY 1	SATURDAY 2	SUNDAY 3

To Do

2022

April

One thing I have desired of the LORD,
That will I seek:
That I may dwell in the house of the LORD
All the days of my life,
To behold the beauty of the LORD,
And to inquire in His temple.

PSALM 27:4 NKJV

My Goals for the Month

APRIL AT A GLANCE

Sun	Mon	Tue	Wed	Thu	Fri	Sat
					1	2
3	4	5	6	7	8	9
10	11	12	13	14	15	16
17	18	19	20	21	22	23
24	25	26	27	28	29	30

APRIL

APRIL 2022

S	M	T	W	T	F	S
					1	2
3	4	5	6	7	8	9
10	11	12	13	14	15	16
17	18	19	20	21	22	23
24	25	26	27	28	29	30

MAY 2022

S	M	T	W	T	F	S
1	2	3	4	5	6	7
8	9	10	11	12	13	14
15	16	17	18	19	20	21
22	23	24	25	26	27	28
29	30	31				

Prayer List	MONDAY 4	TUESDAY 5	WEDNESDAY 6

Priorities

I'm thankful for...

You saw me before I was born.
Every day of my life was recorded
in your book.
Every moment was laid out
before a single day had passed.

PSALM 139:16 NLT

THURSDAY 7	FRIDAY 8	SATURDAY 9	SUNDAY 10

APRIL

APRIL 2022

S	M	T	W	T	F	S
					1	2
3	4	5	6	7	8	9
10	11	12	13	14	15	16
17	18	19	20	21	22	23
24	25	26	27	28	29	30

MAY 2022

S	M	T	W	T	F	S
1	2	3	4	5	6	7
8	9	10	11	12	13	14
15	16	17	18	19	20	21
22	23	24	25	26	27	28
29	30	31				

Prayer List

MONDAY 11

TUESDAY 12

WEDNESDAY 13

Priorities

I'm thankful for...

When we obey him,
every path he guides us on
is fragrant with his loving-kindness
and his truth.

PSALM 25:10 TLB

THURSDAY 14	FRIDAY 15	SATURDAY 16	SUNDAY 17

APRIL

APRIL 2022						
S	M	T	W	T	F	S
					1	2
3	4	5	6	7	8	9
10	11	12	13	14	15	16
17	18	19	20	21	22	23
24	25	26	27	28	29	30

MAY 2022						
S	M	T	W	T	F	S
1	2	3	4	5	6	7
8	9	10	11	12	13	14
15	16	17	18	19	20	21
22	23	24	25	26	27	28
29	30	31				

Prayer List	MONDAY 18	TUESDAY 19	WEDNESDAY 20

Priorities

I'm thankful for...

This is the day the LORD has made;
We will rejoice and be glad in it.

PSALM 118:24 NKJV

THURSDAY 21	FRIDAY 22	SATURDAY 23	SUNDAY 24

APRIL/ MAY

APRIL 2022						
S	M	T	W	T	F	S
					1	2
3	4	5	6	7	8	9
10	11	12	13	14	15	16
17	18	19	20	21	22	23
24	25	26	27	28	29	30

MAY 2022						
S	M	T	W	T	F	S
1	2	3	4	5	6	7
8	9	10	11	12	13	14
15	16	17	18	19	20	21
22	23	24	25	26	27	28
29	30	31				

Prayer List

MONDAY 25

TUESDAY 26

WEDNESDAY 27

Priorities

I'm thankful for...

I remember what happened long ago;
I consider everything you have done.
I think about all you have made.

PSALM 143:5 NCV

THURSDAY 28	FRIDAY 29	SATURDAY 30	SUNDAY 1

To Do

2022

May

Be truly glad! There is wonderful joy ahead....
You love him even though you have never seen him.
Though you do not see him now, you trust him;
and you rejoice with a glorious, inexpressible joy.

1 PETER 1:6, 8 NLT

My Goals for the Month

MAY AT A GLANCE

Sun	Mon	Tue	Wed	Thu	Fri	Sat
1	2	3	4	5	6	7
8	9	10	11	12	13	14
15	16	17	18	19	20	21
22	23	24	25	26	27	28
29	30	31				

MAY

MAY 2022						
S	M	T	W	T	F	S
1	2	3	4	5	6	7
8	9	10	11	12	13	14
15	16	17	18	19	20	21
22	23	24	25	26	27	28
29	30	31				

JUNE 2022						
S	M	T	W	T	F	S
			1	2	3	4
5	6	7	8	9	10	11
12	13	14	15	16	17	18
19	20	21	22	23	24	25
26	27	28	29	30		

Prayer List

MONDAY 2

TUESDAY 3

WEDNESDAY 4

Priorities

I'm thankful for...

Ever since the world was created,
people have seen the earth and sky.
Through everything God made,
they can clearly see his invisible
qualities—his eternal power
and divine nature.

ROMANS 1:20 NLT

THURSDAY 5	FRIDAY 6	SATURDAY 7	SUNDAY 8

MAY

MAY 2022						
S	M	T	W	T	F	S
1	2	3	4	5	6	7
8	9	10	11	12	13	14
15	16	17	18	19	20	21
22	23	24	25	26	27	28
29	30	31				

JUNE 2022						
S	M	T	W	T	F	S
			1	2	3	4
5	6	7	8	9	10	11
12	13	14	15	16	17	18
19	20	21	22	23	24	25
26	27	28	29	30		

Prayer List	MONDAY 9	TUESDAY 10	WEDNESDAY 11

Priorities

I'm thankful for...

"I am leaving you with a gift—
peace of mind and heart.
And the peace I give is a gift
the world cannot give.
So don't be troubled or afraid."

JOHN 14:27 NLT

THURSDAY 12	FRIDAY 13	SATURDAY 14	SUNDAY 15

MAY

MAY 2022						
S	M	T	W	T	F	S
1	2	3	4	5	6	7
8	9	10	11	12	13	14
15	16	17	18	19	20	21
22	23	24	25	26	27	28
29	30	31				

JUNE 2022						
S	M	T	W	T	F	S
			1	2	3	4
5	6	7	8	9	10	11
12	13	14	15	16	17	18
19	20	21	22	23	24	25
26	27	28	29	30		

Prayer List

MONDAY 16

TUESDAY 17

WEDNESDAY 18

Priorities

I'm thankful for...

Let all that I am praise the LORD;
may I never forget the good things
he does for me.

PSALM 103:2 NLT

THURSDAY 19	FRIDAY 20	SATURDAY 21	SUNDAY 22

MAY

MAY 2022						
S	M	T	W	T	F	S
1	2	3	4	5	6	7
8	9	10	11	12	13	14
15	16	17	18	19	20	21
22	23	24	25	26	27	28
29	30	31				

JUNE 2022						
S	M	T	W	T	F	S
			1	2	3	4
5	6	7	8	9	10	11
12	13	14	15	16	17	18
19	20	21	22	23	24	25
26	27	28	29	30		

Prayer List

MONDAY 23

TUESDAY 24

WEDNESDAY 25

Priorities

I'm thankful for...

"Do not fear, for I am with you;
Do not anxiously look about you,
for I am your God.
I will strengthen you,
surely I will help you."

ISAIAH 41:10 NASB

THURSDAY 26	FRIDAY 27	SATURDAY 28	SUNDAY 29

To Do

2022

June

Praise the LORD!
Praise God in his sanctuary;
praise him in his mighty heavens!
Praise him for his mighty deeds;
praise him according to his excellent greatness!
Let everything that has breath praise the LORD!
Praise the LORD!

PSALM 150:1-2, 6 ESV

My Goals for the Month

JUNE AT A GLANCE

Sun	Mon	Tue	Wed	Thu	Fri	Sat
			1	2	3	4
5	6	7	8	9	10	11
12	13	14	15	16	17	18
19	20	21	22	23	24	25
26	27	28	29	30		

MAY/ JUNE

JUNE 2022						
S	M	T	W	T	F	S
			1	2	3	4
5	6	7	8	9	10	11
12	13	14	15	16	17	18
19	20	21	22	23	24	25
26	27	28	29	30		

JULY 2022						
S	M	T	W	T	F	S
					1	2
3	4	5	6	7	8	9
10	11	12	13	14	15	16
17	18	19	20	21	22	23
24	25	26	27	28	29	30
31						

Prayer List

MONDAY 30

TUESDAY 31

WEDNESDAY 1

Priorities

I'm thankful for...

Those who live in the shelter
of the Most High
will find rest in the shadow
of the Almighty.

PSALM 91:1 NLT

THURSDAY 2	FRIDAY 3	SATURDAY 4	SUNDAY 5

JUNE

JUNE 2022

S	M	T	W	T	F	S
			1	2	3	4
5	6	7	8	9	10	11
12	13	14	15	16	17	18
19	20	21	22	23	24	25
26	27	28	29	30		

JULY 2022

S	M	T	W	T	F	S
					1	2
3	4	5	6	7	8	9
10	11	12	13	14	15	16
17	18	19	20	21	22	23
24	25	26	27	28	29	30
31						

Prayer List	MONDAY 6	TUESDAY 7	WEDNESDAY 8

Priorities

I'm thankful for...

The Lord will keep you
from all harm—
he will watch over your life.

PSALM 121:7 NIV

THURSDAY 9	FRIDAY 10	SATURDAY 11	SUNDAY 12

JUNE

JUNE 2022

S	M	T	W	T	F	S
			1	2	3	4
5	6	7	8	9	10	11
12	13	14	15	16	17	18
19	20	21	22	23	24	25
26	27	28	29	30		

JULY 2022

S	M	T	W	T	F	S
					1	2
3	4	5	6	7	8	9
10	11	12	13	14	15	16
17	18	19	20	21	22	23
24	25	26	27	28	29	30
31						

Prayer List

MONDAY 13

TUESDAY 14

WEDNESDAY 15

Priorities

I'm thankful for...

The heavens are yours;
the earth also is yours;
the world and all that is in it,
you have founded them.

PSALM 89:11 ESV

THURSDAY 16	FRIDAY 17	SATURDAY 18	SUNDAY 19

JUNE

JUNE 2022

S	M	T	W	T	F	S
			1	2	3	4
5	6	7	8	9	10	11
12	13	14	15	16	17	18
19	20	21	22	23	24	25
26	27	28	29	30		

JULY 2022

S	M	T	W	T	F	S
					1	2
3	4	5	6	7	8	9
10	11	12	13	14	15	16
17	18	19	20	21	22	23
24	25	26	27	28	29	30
31						

Prayer List

MONDAY 20

TUESDAY 21

WEDNESDAY 22

Priorities

I'm thankful for...

"You are worthy, our Lord and God,
to receive glory and honor and power,
for you created all things,
and by your will they were created
and have their being."

REVELATION 4:11 NIV

THURSDAY 23	FRIDAY 24	SATURDAY 25	SUNDAY 26

JUNE/ JULY

JUNE 2022						
S	M	T	W	T	F	S
			1	2	3	4
5	6	7	8	9	10	11
12	13	14	15	16	17	18
19	20	21	22	23	24	25
26	27	28	29	30		

JULY 2022						
S	M	T	W	T	F	S
					1	2
3	4	5	6	7	8	9
10	11	12	13	14	15	16
17	18	19	20	21	22	23
24	25	26	27	28	29	30
31						

Prayer List

MONDAY 27

TUESDAY 28

WEDNESDAY 29

Priorities

I'm thankful for...

Praise him, sun and moon;
praise him, all you shining stars.
Praise him, you highest heavens
and you waters above the skies.

PSALM 148:3-5 NIV

THURSDAY 30	FRIDAY 1	SATURDAY 2	SUNDAY 3

To Do

2022

July

O Lord, You have searched me and known me.
You know my sitting down and my rising up;
You understand my thought afar off.
You comprehend my path and my lying down,
And are acquainted with all my ways.
For there is not a word on my tongue,
But behold, O Lord, You know it altogether.

PSALM 139:1-4 NKJV

My Goals for the Month

JULY AT A GLANCE

Sun	Mon	Tue	Wed	Thu	Fri	Sat
					1	2
3	4	5	6	7	8	9
10	11	12	13	14	15	16
17	18	19	20	21	22	23
24 / 31	25	26	27	28	29	30

JULY

JULY 2022						
S	M	T	W	T	F	S
					1	2
3	4	5	6	7	8	9
10	11	12	13	14	15	16
17	18	19	20	21	22	23
24	25	26	27	28	29	30
31						

AUGUST 2022						
S	M	T	W	T	F	S
	1	2	3	4	5	6
7	8	9	10	11	12	13
14	15	16	17	18	19	20
21	22	23	24	25	26	27
28	29	30	31			

Prayer List

MONDAY 4

TUESDAY 5

WEDNESDAY 6

Priorities

I'm thankful for...

The life of every living thing
is in his hand,
and the breath
of every human being.

JOB 12:10 NLT

THURSDAY 7	FRIDAY 8	SATURDAY 9	SUNDAY 10

JULY

JULY 2022						
S	M	T	W	T	F	S
					1	2
3	4	5	6	7	8	9
10	11	12	13	14	15	16
17	18	19	20	21	22	23
24	25	26	27	28	29	30
31						

AUGUST 2022						
S	M	T	W	T	F	S
	1	2	3	4	5	6
7	8	9	10	11	12	13
14	15	16	17	18	19	20
21	22	23	24	25	26	27
28	29	30	31			

Prayer List

MONDAY 11

TUESDAY 12

WEDNESDAY 13

Priorities

I'm thankful for...

He loves righteousness and justice;
The earth is full of the goodness
of the LORD.

PSALM 33:5 NKJV

THURSDAY 14	FRIDAY 15	SATURDAY 16	SUNDAY 17

JULY

JULY 2022						
S	M	T	W	T	F	S
					1	2
3	4	5	6	7	8	9
10	11	12	13	14	15	16
17	18	19	20	21	22	23
24	25	26	27	28	29	30
31						

AUGUST 2022						
S	M	T	W	T	F	S
	1	2	3	4	5	6
7	8	9	10	11	12	13
14	15	16	17	18	19	20
21	22	23	24	25	26	27
28	29	30	31			

Prayer List

MONDAY 18

TUESDAY 19

WEDNESDAY 20

Priorities

I'm thankful for...

The LORD is my shepherd;
I shall not want.
He makes me lie down
in green pastures.

PSALM 23:2 ESV

THURSDAY 21	FRIDAY 22	SATURDAY 23	SUNDAY 24

JULY

JULY 2022						
S	M	T	W	T	F	S
					1	2
3	4	5	6	7	8	9
10	11	12	13	14	15	16
17	18	19	20	21	22	23
24	25	26	27	28	29	30
31						

AUGUST 2022						
S	M	T	W	T	F	S
	1	2	3	4	5	6
7	8	9	10	11	12	13
14	15	16	17	18	19	20
21	22	23	24	25	26	27
28	29	30	31			

Prayer List

MONDAY 25

TUESDAY 26

WEDNESDAY 27

Priorities

I'm thankful for...

The Lord directs the steps
of the godly.
He delights in every detail
of their lives.

PSALM 37:23 NLT

THURSDAY 28	FRIDAY 29	SATURDAY 30	SUNDAY 31

To Do

2022

August

You keep him in perfect peace
whose mind is stayed on you,
because he trusts in you.

ISAIAH 26:3 ESV

My Goals for the Month

....

....

....

....

....

AUGUST AT A GLANCE

Sun	Mon	Tue	Wed	Thu	Fri	Sat
	1	2	3	4	5	6
7	8	9	10	11	12	13
14	15	16	17	18	19	20
21	22	23	24	25	26	27
28	29	30	31			

AUGUST

AUGUST 2022

S	M	T	W	T	F	S
	1	2	3	4	5	6
7	8	9	10	11	12	13
14	15	16	17	18	19	20
21	22	23	24	25	26	27
28	29	30	31			

SEPTEMBER 2022

S	M	T	W	T	F	S
				1	2	3
4	5	6	7	8	9	10
11	12	13	14	15	16	17
18	19	20	21	22	23	24
25	26	27	28	29	30	

Prayer List

MONDAY 1

TUESDAY 2

WEDNESDAY 3

Priorities

I'm thankful for...

Trust in the Lord with all your heart;
do not depend on
your own understanding.

PROVERBS 3:5 NLT

THURSDAY 4	FRIDAY 5	SATURDAY 6	SUNDAY 7

AUGUST

AUGUST 2022						
S	M	T	W	T	F	S
	1	2	3	4	5	6
7	8	9	10	11	12	13
14	15	16	17	18	19	20
21	22	23	24	25	26	27
28	29	30	31			

SEPTEMBER 2022						
S	M	T	W	T	F	S
				1	2	3
4	5	6	7	8	9	10
11	12	13	14	15	16	17
18	19	20	21	22	23	24
25	26	27	28	29	30	

Prayer List

MONDAY 8

TUESDAY 9

WEDNESDAY 10

Priorities

I'm thankful for...

"Yours, O LORD, is the greatness
and the power and the glory
and the victory and the majesty,
for all that is in the heavens
and in the earth is yours."

1 CHRONICLES 29:11 ESV

THURSDAY 11	FRIDAY 12	SATURDAY 13	SUNDAY 14

AUGUST

AUGUST 2022						
S	M	T	W	T	F	S
	1	2	3	4	5	6
7	8	9	10	11	12	13
14	15	16	17	18	19	20
21	22	23	24	25	26	27
28	29	30	31			

SEPTEMBER 2022						
S	M	T	W	T	F	S
				1	2	3
4	5	6	7	8	9	10
11	12	13	14	15	16	17
18	19	20	21	22	23	24
25	26	27	28	29	30	

Prayer List

MONDAY 15

TUESDAY 16

WEDNESDAY 17

Priorities

I'm thankful for...

The Lord is near to all
who call upon Him,
To all who call upon Him in truth.

PSALM 145:18 NKJV

THURSDAY 18	FRIDAY 19	SATURDAY 20	SUNDAY 21

AUGUST

AUGUST 2022

S	M	T	W	T	F	S
	1	2	3	4	5	6
7	8	9	10	11	12	13
14	15	16	17	18	19	20
21	22	23	24	25	26	27
28	29	30	31			

SEPTEMBER 2022

S	M	T	W	T	F	S
				1	2	3
4	5	6	7	8	9	10
11	12	13	14	15	16	17
18	19	20	21	22	23	24
25	26	27	28	29	30	

Prayer List

MONDAY 22

TUESDAY 23

WEDNESDAY 24

Priorities

I'm thankful for...

"His purpose was for the nations to seek after God and perhaps feel their way toward him and find him—though he is not far from any one of us."

ACTS 17:27 NLT

THURSDAY 25	FRIDAY 26	SATURDAY 27	SUNDAY 28

To Do

2022

September

Surely you have granted him unending blessings
and made him glad with the joy of your presence.

PSALM 21:6 NIV

My Goals for the Month

SEPTEMBER AT A GLANCE

Sun	Mon	Tue	Wed	Thu	Fri	Sat
				1	2	3
4	5	6	7	8	9	10
11	12	13	14	15	16	17
18	19	20	21	22	23	24
25	26	27	28	29	30	

AUGUST/ SEPTEMBER

SEPTEMBER 2022

S	M	T	W	T	F	S
				1	2	3
4	5	6	7	8	9	10
11	12	13	14	15	16	17
18	19	20	21	22	23	24
25	26	27	28	29	30	

OCTOBER 2022

S	M	T	W	T	F	S
						1
2	3	4	5	6	7	8
9	10	11	12	13	14	15
16	17	18	19	20	21	22
23	24	25	26	27	28	29
30	31					

Prayer List	MONDAY 29	TUESDAY 30	WEDNESDAY 31

Priorities

I'm thankful for...

Your word is like a lamp for my feet and a light for my path.

PSALM 119:105 NCV

THURSDAY 1	FRIDAY 2	SATURDAY 3	SUNDAY 4

SEPTEMBER

SEPTEMBER 2022						
S	M	T	W	T	F	S
				1	2	3
4	5	6	7	8	9	10
11	12	13	14	15	16	17
18	19	20	21	22	23	24
25	26	27	28	29	30	

OCTOBER 2022						
S	M	T	W	T	F	S
						1
2	3	4	5	6	7	8
9	10	11	12	13	14	15
16	17	18	19	20	21	22
23	24	25	26	27	28	29
30	31					

Prayer List	MONDAY 5	TUESDAY 6	WEDNESDAY 7

Priorities

I'm thankful for...

Bless the Lord, O my soul,
and forget not all his benefits.
Who satisfies you with good
so that your youth is
renewed like the eagle's.

PSALM 103:2, 5 ESV

THURSDAY 8	FRIDAY 9	SATURDAY 10	SUNDAY 11

SEPTEMBER

SEPTEMBER 2022						
S	M	T	W	T	F	S
				1	2	3
4	5	6	7	8	9	10
11	12	13	14	15	16	17
18	19	20	21	22	23	24
25	26	27	28	29	30	

OCTOBER 2022						
S	M	T	W	T	F	S
						1
2	3	4	5	6	7	8
9	10	11	12	13	14	15
16	17	18	19	20	21	22
23	24	25	26	27	28	29
30	31					

Prayer List	MONDAY 12	TUESDAY 13	WEDNESDAY 14

Priorities

I'm thankful for...

Let your roots grow down into him, and let your lives be built on him. Then your faith will grow strong in the truth you were taught, and you will overflow with thankfulness.

COLOSSIANS 2:7 NLT

THURSDAY 15	FRIDAY 16	SATURDAY 17	SUNDAY 18

SEPTEMBER

SEPTEMBER 2022

S	M	T	W	T	F	S
				1	2	3
4	5	6	7	8	9	10
11	12	13	14	15	16	17
18	19	20	21	22	23	24
25	26	27	28	29	30	

OCTOBER 2022

S	M	T	W	T	F	S
						1
2	3	4	5	6	7	8
9	10	11	12	13	14	15
16	17	18	19	20	21	22
23	24	25	26	27	28	29
30	31					

Prayer List	MONDAY 19	TUESDAY 20	WEDNESDAY 21

Priorities

I'm thankful for...

Send out your light and your truth;
let them lead me;
let them bring me to your holy hill
and to your dwelling.

PSALM 43:3 NRSV

THURSDAY 22	FRIDAY 23	SATURDAY 24	SUNDAY 25

SEPTEMBER/ OCTOBER

SEPTEMBER 2022						
S	M	T	W	T	F	S
				1	2	3
4	5	6	7	8	9	10
11	12	13	14	15	16	17
18	19	20	21	22	23	24
25	26	27	28	29	30	

OCTOBER 2022						
S	M	T	W	T	F	S
						1
2	3	4	5	6	7	8
9	10	11	12	13	14	15
16	17	18	19	20	21	22
23	24	25	26	27	28	29
30	31					

Prayer List

MONDAY 26

TUESDAY 27

WEDNESDAY 28

Priorities

I'm thankful for...

Can anything ever separate us from Christ's love? No, despite all these things, overwhelming victory is ours through Christ, who loved us.

ROMANS 8:35, 37 NLT

THURSDAY 29	FRIDAY 30	SATURDAY 1	SUNDAY 2

To Do

2022

October

The Lord will fulfill his purpose for me;
your steadfast love, O Lord, endures forever.
Do not forsake the work of your hands.

PSALM 138:8 ESV

My Goals for the Month

OCTOBER AT A GLANCE

Sun	Mon	Tue	Wed	Thu	Fri	Sat
						1
2	3	4	5	6	7	8
9	10	11	12	13	14	15
16	17	18	19	20	21	22
23 / 30	24 / 31	25	26	27	28	29

OCTOBER

OCTOBER 2022

S	M	T	W	T	F	S
						1
2	3	4	5	6	7	8
9	10	11	12	13	14	15
16	17	18	19	20	21	22
23	24	25	26	27	28	29
30	31					

NOVEMBER 2022

S	M	T	W	T	F	S
		1	2	3	4	5
6	7	8	9	10	11	12
13	14	15	16	17	18	19
20	21	22	23	24	25	26
27	28	29	30			

Prayer List	MONDAY 3	TUESDAY 4	WEDNESDAY 5

Priorities

I'm thankful for...

Listen carefully to wisdom;
set your mind on understanding.
Cry out for wisdom,
and beg for understanding.

PROVERBS 2:2-3 NCV

THURSDAY 6	FRIDAY 7	SATURDAY 8	SUNDAY 9

OCTOBER

OCTOBER 2022

S	M	T	W	T	F	S
						1
2	3	4	5	6	7	8
9	10	11	12	13	14	15
16	17	18	19	20	21	22
23	24	25	26	27	28	29
30	31					

NOVEMBER 2022

S	M	T	W	T	F	S
		1	2	3	4	5
6	7	8	9	10	11	12
13	14	15	16	17	18	19
20	21	22	23	24	25	26
27	28	29	30			

Prayer List	MONDAY 10	TUESDAY 11	WEDNESDAY 12

Priorities

I'm thankful for...

He renews my strength.
He guides me along right paths,
bringing honor to his name.

PSALM 23:3 NLT

THURSDAY 13	FRIDAY 14	SATURDAY 15	SUNDAY 16

OCTOBER

OCTOBER 2022						
S	M	T	W	T	F	S
						1
2	3	4	5	6	7	8
9	10	11	12	13	14	15
16	17	18	19	20	21	22
23	24	25	26	27	28	29
30	31					

NOVEMBER 2022						
S	M	T	W	T	F	S
		1	2	3	4	5
6	7	8	9	10	11	12
13	14	15	16	17	18	19
20	21	22	23	24	25	26
27	28	29	30			

Prayer List

MONDAY 17

TUESDAY 18

WEDNESDAY 19

Priorities

I'm thankful for...

Seek his will in all you do,
and he will show you
which path to take.

PROVERBS 3:6 NLT

THURSDAY 20	FRIDAY 21	SATURDAY 22	SUNDAY 23

OCTOBER

OCTOBER 2022

S	M	T	W	T	F	S
						1
2	3	4	5	6	7	8
9	10	11	12	13	14	15
16	17	18	19	20	21	22
23	24	25	26	27	28	29
30	31					

NOVEMBER 2022

S	M	T	W	T	F	S
		1	2	3	4	5
6	7	8	9	10	11	12
13	14	15	16	17	18	19
20	21	22	23	24	25	26
27	28	29	30			

Prayer List

MONDAY 24

TUESDAY 25

WEDNESDAY 26

Priorities

I'm thankful for...

Thanks be to God
for his inexpressible gift!

2 CORINTHIANS 9:15 ESV

THURSDAY 27	FRIDAY 28	SATURDAY 29	SUNDAY 30

To Do

2022

November

Commit your work to the LORD,
and your plans will be established.

PROVERBS 16:3 ESV

My Goals for the Month

NOVEMBER AT A GLANCE

Sun	Mon	Tue	Wed	Thu	Fri	Sat
		1	2	3	4	5
6	7	8	9	10	11	12
13	14	15	16	17	18	19
20	21	22	23	24	25	26
27	28	29	30			

OCTOBER/ NOVEMBER

NOVEMBER 2022						
S	M	T	W	T	F	S
		1	2	3	4	5
6	7	8	9	10	11	12
13	14	15	16	17	18	19
20	21	22	23	24	25	26
27	28	29	30			

DECEMBER 2022						
S	M	T	W	T	F	S
				1	2	3
4	5	6	7	8	9	10
11	12	13	14	15	16	17
18	19	20	21	22	23	24
25	26	27	28	29	30	31

Prayer List	MONDAY 31	TUESDAY 1	WEDNESDAY 2

Priorities

I'm thankful for...

Every good and perfect gift is from above, coming down from the Father of the heavenly lights, who does not change like shifting shadows.

JAMES 1:17 NIV

THURSDAY 3	FRIDAY 4	SATURDAY 5	SUNDAY 6

NOVEMBER

NOVEMBER 2022						
S	M	T	W	T	F	S
		1	2	3	4	5
6	7	8	9	10	11	12
13	14	15	16	17	18	19
20	21	22	23	24	25	26
27	28	29	30			

DECEMBER 2022						
S	M	T	W	T	F	S
				1	2	3
4	5	6	7	8	9	10
11	12	13	14	15	16	17
18	19	20	21	22	23	24
25	26	27	28	29	30	31

Prayer List

MONDAY 7

TUESDAY 8

WEDNESDAY 9

Priorities

I'm thankful for...

I am confident of this very thing, that He who began a good work in you will perfect it until the day of Christ Jesus.

PHILIPPIANS 1:6 NASB

THURSDAY 10	FRIDAY 11	SATURDAY 12	SUNDAY 13

NOVEMBER

NOVEMBER 2022						
S	M	T	W	T	F	S
		1	2	3	4	5
6	7	8	9	10	11	12
13	14	15	16	17	18	19
20	21	22	23	24	25	26
27	28	29	30			

DECEMBER 2022						
S	M	T	W	T	F	S
				1	2	3
4	5	6	7	8	9	10
11	12	13	14	15	16	17
18	19	20	21	22	23	24
25	26	27	28	29	30	31

Prayer List	MONDAY 14	TUESDAY 15	WEDNESDAY 16

Priorities

I'm thankful for...

Yet the LORD longs
to be gracious to you;
therefore he will rise up
to show you compassion.

ISAIAH 30:18 NIV

THURSDAY 17	FRIDAY 18	SATURDAY 19	SUNDAY 20

NOVEMBER

NOVEMBER 2022						
S	M	T	W	T	F	S
		1	2	3	4	5
6	7	8	9	10	11	12
13	14	15	16	17	18	19
20	21	22	23	24	25	26
27	28	29	30			

DECEMBER 2022						
S	M	T	W	T	F	S
				1	2	3
4	5	6	7	8	9	10
11	12	13	14	15	16	17
18	19	20	21	22	23	24
25	26	27	28	29	30	31

Prayer List

MONDAY 21

TUESDAY 22

WEDNESDAY 23

Priorities

I'm thankful for...

Seek to do good to one another and to everyone.

1 THESSALONIANS 5:15 ESV

THURSDAY 24	FRIDAY 25	SATURDAY 26	SUNDAY 27

To Do

2022

December

His divine power has granted to us everything pertaining to life and godliness, through the true knowledge of Him who called us by His own glory and excellence.

2 PETER 1:3 NASB

My Goals for the Month

DECEMBER AT A GLANCE

Sun	Mon	Tue	Wed	Thu	Fri	Sat
				1	2	3
4	5	6	7	8	9	10
11	12	13	14	15	16	17
18	19	20	21	22	23	24
25	26	27	28	29	30	31

NOVEMBER/ DECEMBER

DECEMBER 2022						
S	M	T	W	T	F	S
				1	2	3
4	5	6	7	8	9	10
11	12	13	14	15	16	17
18	19	20	21	22	23	24
25	26	27	28	29	30	31

JANUARY 2023						
S	M	T	W	T	F	S
1	2	3	4	5	6	7
8	9	10	11	12	13	14
15	16	17	18	19	20	21
22	23	24	25	26	27	28
29	30	31				

Prayer List

MONDAY 28

TUESDAY 29

WEDNESDAY 30

Priorities

I'm thankful for...

The LORD has told you what is good,
and this is what he requires of you:
to do what is right, to love mercy,
and to walk humbly with your God.

MICAH 6:8 NLT

THURSDAY 1	FRIDAY 2	SATURDAY 3	SUNDAY 4

DECEMBER

DECEMBER 2022						
S	M	T	W	T	F	S
				1	2	3
4	5	6	7	8	9	10
11	12	13	14	15	16	17
18	19	20	21	22	23	24
25	26	27	28	29	30	31

JANUARY 2023						
S	M	T	W	T	F	S
1	2	3	4	5	6	7
8	9	10	11	12	13	14
15	16	17	18	19	20	21
22	23	24	25	26	27	28
29	30	31				

Prayer List	MONDAY 5	TUESDAY 6	WEDNESDAY 7

Priorities

I'm thankful for...

"Come to me,
all you who are weary and burdened,
and I will give you rest."

MATTHEW 11:28 NIV

THURSDAY 8	FRIDAY 9	SATURDAY 10	SUNDAY 11

DECEMBER

DECEMBER 2022

S	M	T	W	T	F	S
				1	2	3
4	5	6	7	8	9	10
11	12	13	14	15	16	17
18	19	20	21	22	23	24
25	26	27	28	29	30	31

JANUARY 2023

S	M	T	W	T	F	S
1	2	3	4	5	6	7
8	9	10	11	12	13	14
15	16	17	18	19	20	21
22	23	24	25	26	27	28
29	30	31				

Prayer List

MONDAY 12

TUESDAY 13

WEDNESDAY 14

Priorities

I'm thankful for...

Jesus Christ is the same yesterday
and today and forever.

HEBREWS 13:8 NASB

THURSDAY 15	FRIDAY 16	SATURDAY 17	SUNDAY 18

DECEMBER

DECEMBER 2022						
S	M	T	W	T	F	S
				1	2	3
4	5	6	7	8	9	10
11	12	13	14	15	16	17
18	19	20	21	22	23	24
25	26	27	28	29	30	31

JANUARY 2023						
S	M	T	W	T	F	S
1	2	3	4	5	6	7
8	9	10	11	12	13	14
15	16	17	18	19	20	21
22	23	24	25	26	27	28
29	30	31				

Prayer List

MONDAY 19

TUESDAY 20

WEDNESDAY 21

Priorities

I'm thankful for...

Cast all your anxiety on him,
because he cares for you.

1 PETER 5:7 NRSV

THURSDAY 22	FRIDAY 23	SATURDAY 24	SUNDAY 25

DECEMBER/ JANUARY

DECEMBER 2022						
S	M	T	W	T	F	S
				1	2	3
4	5	6	7	8	9	10
11	12	13	14	15	16	17
18	19	20	21	22	23	24
25	26	27	28	29	30	31

JANUARY 2023						
S	M	T	W	T	F	S
1	2	3	4	5	6	7
8	9	10	11	12	13	14
15	16	17	18	19	20	21
22	23	24	25	26	27	28
29	30	31				

Prayer List

MONDAY 26

TUESDAY 27

WEDNESDAY 28

Priorities

I'm thankful for...

For God has not given us
a spirit of fear, but of power
and of love and of a sound mind.

2 TIMOTHY 1:7 NKJV

THURSDAY 29	FRIDAY 30	SATURDAY 31	SUNDAY 1

To Do

Bible Promises

ABILITY

We are not saying that we can do this work ourselves. It is God who makes us able to do all that we do.

2 Corinthians 3:5 NCV

Take a new grip with your tired hands and strengthen your weak knees. Mark out a straight path for your feet so that those who are weak and lame will not fall but become strong.

Hebrews 12:12-13 NLT

"My grace is sufficient for you, for my power is made perfect in weakness." Therefore I will boast all the more gladly of my weaknesses, so that the power of Christ may rest upon me.

2 Corinthians 12:9 ESV

ACCEPTANCE

"The Father gives me the people who are mine. Every one of them will come to me, and I will always accept them."

John 6:37 NCV

Before he made the world, God chose us to be his very own through what Christ would do for us; he decided then to make us holy in his eyes, without a single fault—we who stand before him covered with his love.

Ephesians 1:4 TLB

ANGER

A gentle answer deflects anger,
but harsh words make tempers flare.

Proverbs 15:1 NLT

In your hearts revere Christ as Lord. Always be prepared to give an answer to everyone who asks you to give the reason for the hope that you have. But do this with gentleness and respect.

1 Peter 3:15 NIV

"Blessed are the gentle, for they shall inherit the earth."
Matthew 5:5 NASB

Let your gentleness be evident to all. The Lord is near.
Philippians 4:5 NIV

ANXIETY

"Do not let not your hearts be troubled. Believe in God, believe also in me."
John 14:1 NRSV

Cast all your anxiety on him because he cares for you.
1 Peter 5:7 NIV

Be still, and know that I am God.
I will be exalted among the nations,
I will be exalted in the earth!
Psalm 46:10 ESV

Do not be anxious about anything, but in every situation, by prayer and petition, with thanksgiving, present your requests to God.
Philippians 4:6 NIV

ASSURANCE

Your promises have been thoroughly tested,
and your servant loves them.
My eyes stay open through the watches of the night,
that I may meditate on your promises.
Psalm 119:140, 148 NIV

He has granted to us his precious and very great promises, so that through them you may become partakers of the divine nature, having escaped from the corruption that is in the world.
2 Peter 1:3-4 ESV

To him who is able to do immeasurably more than all we ask or imagine, according to his power that is at work within us, to him be glory...for ever and ever! Amen.
Ephesians 3:20–21 NIV

COMFORT

I will give them a crown to replace their ashes,
and the oil of gladness to replace their sorrow,
and clothes of praise to replace their spirit of sadness.
Then they will be called Trees of Goodness,
trees planted by the LORD to show his greatness.

Isaiah 61:3 NCV

May your unfailing love be my comfort,
according to your promise to your servant.

Psalm 119:76 NIV

May our Lord Jesus Christ himself and God our Father, who loved us and by his grace gave us eternal comfort and a wonderful hope, comfort you and strengthen you.

2 Thessalonians 2:16–17 NLT

CONFIDENCE

Be my rock of refuge,
to which I can always go;
give the command to save me,
for you are my rock and my fortress.
You have been my hope, Sovereign LORD,
my confidence since my youth.

Psalm 71:3, 5 NIV

This is the confidence that we have toward him, that if we ask anything according to his will he hears us. And if we know that he hears us in whatever we ask, we know that we have the requests that we have asked of him.

1 John 5:14–15 ESV

Let us then approach God's throne of grace with confidence, so that we may receive mercy and find grace to help us in our time of need.

Hebrews 4:16 NIV

COURAGE

So be strong and courageous,
all you who put your hope in the LORD!

Psalm 31:24 NLT

May he give you the power to accomplish all the good things your faith prompts you to do.
2 Thessalonians 1:11 NLT

"Be strong and courageous. Do not be frightened, and do not be dismayed, for the LORD your God is with you wherever you go."
Joshua 1:9 ESV

DILIGENCE

The plans of the diligent lead to profit
as surely as haste leads to poverty.
Proverbs 21:5 NIV

In all the work you are doing, work the best you can. Work as if you were doing it for the Lord, not for people.
Colossians 3:23 NCV

Be diligent in these matters; give yourself wholly to them, so that everyone may see your progress.
1 Timothy 4:15 NIV

ENCOURAGEMENT

The humble will see their God at work and be glad.
Let all who seek God's help be encouraged.
Psalm 69:32 NLT

We do not lose heart, but though our outer man is decaying, yet our inner man is being renewed day by day. For momentary, light affliction is producing for us an eternal weight of glory far beyond all comparison.
2 Corinthians 4:16–17 NASB

Let us consider how to stir up one another to love and good works, not neglecting to meet together, as is the habit of some, but encouraging one another.
Hebrews 10:24–25 ESV

FAITH

Faith is confidence in what we hope for and assurance about what we do not see.
Hebrews 11:1 NIV

Not one word of all the good words which the Lord your God spoke concerning you has failed; all have been fulfilled for you, not one of them has failed.

Joshua 23:14 NASB

Faith comes by hearing, and hearing by the word of God.

Romans 10:17 NKJV

"If you have faith like a grain of mustard seed, you will say to this mountain, 'Move from here to there,' and it will move, and nothing will be impossible for you."

Matthew 17:20 ESV

FEAR

Where God's love is, there is no fear, because God's love drives out fear.

1 John 4:18 NCV

"Don't be afraid, for I am with you.
Don't be discouraged, for I am your God.
I will strengthen you and help you.
I will hold you up with my victorious right hand."

Isaiah 41:10 NLT

The Lord is my light and my salvation;
whom shall I fear?
The Lord is the stronghold of my life;
of whom shall I be afraid?

Psalm 27:1 ESV

FORGIVENESS

For You, Lord, are good, and ready to forgive,
And abundant in mercy to all those who call upon You.

Psalm 86:5 NKJV

As far as the east is from the west,
So far has He removed our transgressions from us.

Psalm 103:12 NASB

If we confess our sins, He is faithful and just to forgive us our sins and to cleanse us from all unrighteousness.

1 John 1:9 NKJV

My sacrifice, O God, is a broken spirit;
a broken and contrite heart
you, God, will not despise.
Psalm 51:17 NIV

FREEDOM

Now that you have been set free from sin and have become slaves of God, the benefit you reap leads to holiness, and the result is eternal life.
Romans 6:22 NIV

"If you hold to my teaching, you are really my disciples. Then you will know the truth, and the truth will set you free."
John 8:31–32 NIV

Christ has truly set us free. Now make sure that you stay free, and don't get tied up again in slavery to the law.
Galatians 5:1 NLT

GUIDANCE

The Lord directs the steps of the godly.
He delights in every detail of their lives.
Though they stumble, they will never fall,
for the Lord holds them by the hand.
Psalm 37:23–24 NLT

We know that all things work together for good to those who love God, to those who are the called according to His purpose.
Romans 8:28 NKJV

We can make our plans,
but the Lord determines our steps.
Proverbs 16:9 NLT

HEALING

He was pierced for our transgressions, he was crushed for our iniquities;
the punishment that brought us peace was on him, and by his wounds we are healed.
Isaiah 53:5 NIV

"Your faith has made you well; go in peace and be healed of your affliction."
Mark 5:34 NASB

My child, pay attention to what I say.
Listen carefully to my words.
Don't lose sight of them.
Let them penetrate deep into your heart,
for they bring life to those who find them,
and healing to their whole body.
Proverbs 4:20–22 NLT

HONESTY

Truthful words stand the test of time,
but lies are soon exposed.
Proverbs 12:19 NLT

"When he, the Spirit of truth, comes, he will guide you into all the truth."
John 16:13 NIV

You desire truth in the innermost being,
And in the hidden part You will make me know wisdom.
Psalm 51:6 NASB

HOPE

The LORD is good to those whose hope is in him,
to the one who seeks him.
Lamentations 3:25 NIV

Blessed be the God and Father of our Lord Jesus Christ! According to his great mercy, he has caused us to be born again to a living hope through the resurrection of Jesus Christ.
1 Peter 1:3 ESV

May the God of hope fill you with all joy and peace as you trust in him, so that you may overflow with hope by the power of the Holy Spirit.
Romans 15:13 NIV

HUMILITY

Humility is the fear of the Lord;
its wages are riches and honor and life.
Proverbs 22:4 NIV

Those who accept correction gain understanding.
Respect for the Lord will teach you wisdom.
If you want to be honored, you must be humble.
Proverbs 15:32–33 NCV

In your relationships with one another, have the same mindset as Christ Jesus: Who, being in very nature God, did not consider equality with God something to be used to his own advantage; rather, he made himself nothing by taking the very nature of a servant, being made in human likeness.
Philippians 2:5-7 NIV

LONELINESS

The Lord is near to all who call on him,
to all who call on him in truth.
Psalm 145:18 NIV

"Here I am! I stand at the door and knock. If anyone hears my voice and opens the door, I will come in and eat with that person, and they with me."
Revelation 3:20 NIV

"Behold, I am with you always, to the end of the age."
Matthew 28:20 ESV

JOY

The Lord has done great things for us,
and we are filled with joy.
Psalm 126:3 NIV

Satisfy us in the morning with your unfailing love,
that we may sing for joy and be glad all our days.
Psalm 90:14 NIV

Be truly glad. There is wonderful joy ahead.... You love him even though you have never seen him. Though you do not see him now, you trust him; and you rejoice with a glorious, inexpressible joy.

1 Peter 1:6, 8 NLT

"Ask and you will receive, and your joy will be complete."

John 16:24 NIV

PATIENCE

As a prisoner for the Lord, then, I urge you to live a life worthy of the calling you have received. Be completely humble and gentle; be patient, bearing with one another in love.

Ephesians 4:1-2 NIV

"They are those who, hearing the word, hold it fast in an honest and good heart, and bear fruit with patience."

Luke 8:15 ESV

Imitate those who through faith and patience inherit what has been promised.

Hebrews 6:12 NIV

PEACE

"These things I have spoken to you, so that in Me you may have peace. In the world you have tribulation, but take courage; I have overcome the world."

John 16:33 NASB

The Lord will give strength to His people;
The Lord will bless His people with peace.

Psalm 29:11 NKJV

"Peace I leave with you; my peace I give you. I do not give to you as the world gives. Do not let your hearts be troubled and do not be afraid."

John 14:27 NIV

PERSEVERANCE

God blesses those who patiently endure testing and temptation. Afterward they will receive the crown of life that God has promised to those who love him.

James 1:12 NLT

Let us not grow weary of doing good, for in due season we will reap,
if we do not give up.
Galatians 6:9 ESV

Consider it pure joy...whenever you face trials of many kinds, because you know that the testing of your faith develops perseverance. Let perseverance finish its work so that you may be mature and complete, not lacking anything.
James 1:2–4 NIV

PROTECTION

The Lord himself goes before you and will be with you;
he will never leave you nor forsake you.
Deuteronomy 31:8 NIV

If you make the Lord your refuge,
if you make the Most High your shelter,
no evil will conquer you;
no plague will come near your home.
For he will order his angels
to protect you wherever you go.
Psalm 91:9–11 NLT

PROVISION

God is able to provide you with every blessing in abundance, so that by always having enough of everything, you may share abundantly in every good work.
2 Corinthians 9:8 NRSV

The Lord is all I need.
He takes care of me.
My share in life has been pleasant;
my part has been beautiful.
Psalm 16:5–6 NCV

Whoever pursues righteousness and love
finds life, prosperity and honor.
Proverbs 21:21 NIV

REWARD

Do not lose the courage you had in the past, which has a great reward. You must hold on, so you can do what God wants and receive what he has promised.

Hebrews 10:35–36 NCV

Watch yourselves, so that you may not lose what we have worked for, but may win a full reward.

2 John 1:8 ESV

"Look, I am coming soon! My reward is with me, and I will give to each person according to what they have done."

Revelation 22:12 NIV

STRENGTH

Whom have I in heaven but you?
And earth has nothing I desire besides you.
My flesh and my heart may fail,
but God is the strength of my heart
and my portion forever.

Psalm 73:25–26 NIV

Live as citizens of heaven, conducting yourselves in a manner worthy of the Good News about Christ...standing together with one spirit and one purpose, fighting together for the faith. Don't be intimidated in any way by your enemies. This will be a sign to them that you are going to be saved, even by God himself.

Philippians 1:27–28 NLT

THANKFULNESS

Thanks be to God for his indescribable gift!

2 Corinthians 9:15 NIV

Always be thankful. Let the message about Christ, in all its richness, fill your lives.

Colossians 3:15 NLT

In everything give thanks; for this is God's will for you in Christ Jesus.

1 Thessalonians 5:18 NASB

WISDOM

If any of you lacks wisdom, you should ask God, who gives generously to all without finding fault, and it will be given to you.

James 1:5 NIV

Be filled with the knowledge of His will in all spiritual wisdom and understanding,
so that you will walk in a manner worthy of the Lord…
and increasing in the knowledge of God.

Colossians 1:9-10 NASB

The wisdom from above is first of all pure. It is also peace loving, gentle at all times, and willing to yield to others. It is full of mercy and good deeds. It shows no favoritism and is always sincere.

James 3:17 NLT

WORRY

"Which of you by worrying can add a single hour to his life's span?"

Luke 12:25 NASB

Don't worry about anything; instead, pray about everything. Tell God what you need, and thank him for all he has done. Then you will experience God's peace, which exceeds anything we can understand. His peace will guard your hearts and minds as you live in Christ Jesus.

Philippians 4:6–7 NLT

Give your burdens to the Lord,
and he will take care of you.

Psalm 55:22 NLT